IMAGES
of America

ST. JOHNSBURY

Dedication

Dedicated, with admiration, to the fine photographers who recorded
these images of St. Johnsbury, and by doing so preserved for us the people, places,
and ways of life that would otherwise have been lost forever.

ST. JOHNSBURY HOSPITAL. St. Johnsbury Hospital, the first such institution in town, was built in 1895 through the efforts of Father J.A. Boissonnault, pastor of our local Roman Catholic parish, Notre Dame des Victoires. It was staffed by the Sisters of Providence, from Montreal, and provided fine nursing for many years.

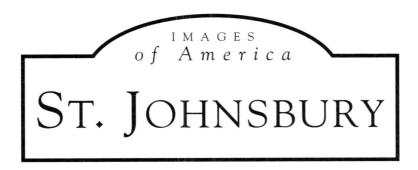

IMAGES
of America

ST. JOHNSBURY

Claire Dunne Johnson

ARCADIA

First published 1996
Copyright © Claire Dunne Johnson, 1996

ISBN 0-7524-0260-9

Published by Arcadia Publishing,
an imprint of the Chalford Publishing Corporation
One Washington Center, Dover, New Hampshire 03820
Printed in Great Britain

Library of Congress Cataloging-in-Publication Data applied for

Contents

Acknowledgments

This book couldn't have been published without the gracious contributions of many St. Johnsbury people. Mark M. Smith, publisher of the *Caledonian-Record*, permitted the use of photographs from the newspaper's archives, and Wayland Sinclair made prints from those negatives. Director Perry Viles and librarian Lisa von Kann of the Athenaeum provided photographs, as did the Fairbanks Museum. Those of the St. Johnsbury Trucking Company came from the John Simons collection; and Archie Prevost, a retired CP railroad engineer, submitted many others depicting the community's busier railroading days. Peggy Pearl, president of the St. Johnsbury Historical Society, Howard Reed, Martin Bryan, Gerry Heon, Graham Newell, Julian Butler, and Ron Wilkie were all helpful in identifying, dating, and selecting the photographs for publication. Martin, who did much of the "legwork," was a valuable assistant in the decision-making process. My husband, Jerry, helped with some needed photo enhancement, in a temporary darkroom. Such cooperation and generosity was greatly appreciated.

Introduction

When the idea of putting together a photographic history of St. Johnsbury was first suggested in the fall of 1995, it seemed like an idea with interesting possibilities. Peggy Pearl, Martin Bryan, and I had all been contacted, because of our historical society connections, and after a meeting with the senior editor of Arcadia Publishing, we decided to go ahead with the project. Since Peggy and Martin had a living to make, while I was comfortably retired, the authoring efforts came to be mine.

The knowledge that we would need some two hundred pictures for the book was somewhat daunting. We knew that St. Johnsbury was much more fortunate than many places, in terms of having institutions that had carefully preserved historical artifacts as a part of their contribution to the town. Horace Fairbanks' Athenaeum had long been collecting articles and materials involved in the growth and development of St. Johnsbury. This included many, many photographs, which had for a long time been in a somewhat disorganized state. As luck would have it, these had quite recently been arranged and indexed in very usable album style by the efforts of Gerry Heon, and we are very grateful for his dedication to that job. The Fairbanks Museum, also, was most generous with access to its hundreds of pictures, and we profited immeasurably from its collections.

All of this historical material was a tremendous resource for the earlier years of the 1860-to-1960 time period which the book covers. One feels sure that both Horace and Franklin would have thoroughly approved of this way to share the treasure houses of historical information that they had helped to preserve for the people of St. Johnsbury.

However, it did not take long to realize that there was a problem in getting material for more recent years. Our fine early photographers, F.B. Gage and D.A. Clifford, had passed from the scene much too soon. We did have two fine replacements to give us some helpful views through the first part of the twentieth century—Katherine Bingham and Amelia Perham, whose prize-winning photography brought recognition to them as well as to St. Johnsbury. However, we still had a long way to go to reach 1960.

Then someone said, "What about the *Caledonian-Record*? Wouldn't they have pictures?" They, of course, had been taking photographs ever since the advent of Ernie Evans, their full-time photographer, in 1946; but were those available? Martin Bryan contacted Mark M. Smith, the publisher, and found him most willing to share the archives—always provided that we could sort out what we wanted from the somewhat confused jumble which had ended up in the old darkroom closet.

This was a challenge that Martin handled most admirably. He hauled out cartons, hunted for identifying dates, and eventually brought over to me all of the years from 1947 to 1960. These were all negatives, you understand, and not photographs to look at and recognize. And so we started working our way through them, with the use of a homemade light box, while electronically reversing the negative images. This was fascinating, of course, but along with the fun was the monumental task of sorting and alphabetizing the individual folders of pictures taken at each scene. Eventually we got them all in neat order, so that they could be easily located.

There was another problem. We had dozens of negatives that we wanted prints of, and that is an expensive business. Mark Smith came to the rescue again. "Sure," he said, "We can print those for you." What a relief! And so we are very grateful, also, to Wayland Sinclair, who put in much extra effort.

After finding solutions to these problems, only one rather major detail remained—we had dozens of pictures, and we didn't have room for quantities like that. This boiled down to having to make difficult choices. I think if there is anything worse than not having enough pictures, it is having too many and needing to leave some out which you really hate not to use. Ah, well— we have done the best we could.

St. Johnsbury is a very fine town. Yes, it is my home town and I may be a bit prejudiced, but one has only to take a look at the unusual advantages which we enjoy to realize how fortunate we have always been and still are. Thaddeus Fairbanks' platform scale started us on the way to growth and progress, with a factory that provided jobs for hundreds of area people. His brother Erastus, twice governor of Vermont, managed to get the north-south railroad line through St. Johnsbury, and his nephew Horace accomplished the difficult task of getting an east-west rail line built from Portland through Vermont to Lake Champlain, by way of St. Johnsbury.

The Fairbanks business made a lot of money, and the family gave much of it back to St. Johnsbury in the form of cultural institutions which much larger towns and cities could envy. Our Athenaeum and Museum, which we sometimes take for granted because we have grown up with them, amaze visitors who cannot imagine such riches of art and science in a town of this size, located way up in northern Vermont. We do have other advantages, too—our location at the intersection of two interstate highways, for instance. But perhaps the one which I personally enjoy the most is our uncanny luck in being just on the fringe of the nastiest snowstorms, thunderstorms, and windstorms, tucked away safely in our little valley. I do like St. Johnsbury.

One
Made in
St. Johnsbury

FAIRBANKS & CO., 1890. No one would question that one product made in St. Johnsbury was a vital factor in stimulating the growth of the town. The Fairbanks platform scale, invented in 1830 by Thaddeus Fairbanks, became so demanded worldwide, through the years, that the factory here grew to major proportions and provided hundreds of jobs to people in the area.

FAIRBANKS' WORKERS IN MECHANIC SQUARE, late 1860s. The home of Governor Erastus Fairbanks can be seen behind this gathering of the Fairbanks' employees in what was called Mechanic Square, in front of the factory. In 1870 the buildings in the left rear were removed to be replaced by the familiar brick office building and, later, the Fairbanks' grocery store.

FINISHING FAIRBANKS' BIG CHIMNEY, 1891. In June 1891, this huge chimney, the largest in the state of Vermont, was completed. These brick masons posed triumphantly at the top, far above the rest of the world. One of them is Silas Masten, who laid the final brick to complete the job.

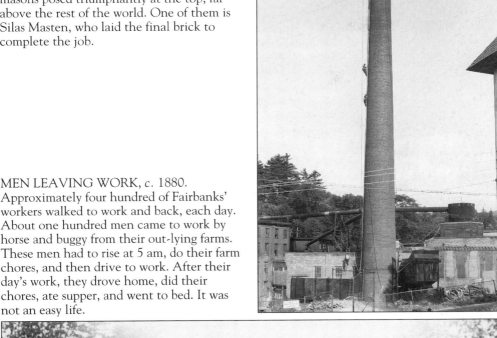

MEN LEAVING WORK, *c.* 1880. Approximately four hundred of Fairbanks' workers walked to work and back, each day. About one hundred men came to work by horse and buggy from their out-lying farms. These men had to rise at 5 am, do their farm chores, and then drive to work. After their day's work, they drove home, did their chores, ate supper, and went to bed. It was not an easy life.

THE FAIRBANKS' LUMBER YARD AND HORSE BARN, 1885. Fairbanks' large lumber yard was a busy place. The factory used three million board feet of lumber annually, mainly to box scales for shipment. The big barn on Clay Hill housed a large number of their horses.

THE INTERIOR OF FAIRBANKS' GROCERY STORE, 1890s. The original grocery store was destroyed by fire in 1889, and the new one was completed and opened in November 1890. This was a company store, carrying a wide range of goods which the workers could buy on credit. What they owed was deducted from their monthly pay envelopes, which were delivered to them at their work posts.

THE ELY HOE & FORK CO. BUILDING, 1900. This fine brick building, using power from a high dam on the Moose River off Portland Street, was the third factory structure built by George Ely, who began his hoe and fork manufactory in 1849 and saw it twice destroyed by fire.

ELY EMPLOYEES, c. 1910. These men turned out forks and hoes of such quality that they won acclaim over a wide area. The flexibility and spring of the fork tines won prizes at fairs and expositions as far away as Wisconsin, Michigan, and Missouri.

THE ELY WORKS, TRUE TEMPER CORPORATION, 1949. The Ely plant, which since 1902 had been a part of American Fork & Hoe, was taken over by the large True-Temper Corporation in 1949. The supply of ash logs which kept the plant in business here was still ample when this photograph was taken.

IDE COAL WAGONS, 1920. The E.T. & H.K. Ide Co. did a thriving business in coal, delivering it to homes in wagons during the spring, summer, and fall, and in sleighs during the winter. Hopping onto the Ide sleigh runners and catching a ride up Portland Street to school was a popular, though forbidden, pastime.

THE E.T. & H.K. IDE CO., 1910. The Ide Co. is one of the oldest family-owned businesses in the state, having been in continuous operation since 1813. These Bay Street buildings were built in 1906. The elevator is 50 feet high, and the circular building is a corn bin capable of holding 12,000 bushels.

THE E.T. & H.K. IDE CO. PLANT, *c.* 1950. The Ide Co. made good use of our excellent rail transportation to bring in their grain supply from the West. This is one of the St. Johnsbury & Lake Champlain locomotives which operated in the rail yard. In the background is the fine overpass completed in 1943 as a part of what was called the Federal Aid Strategic Network, for military transportation. It spans the Passumpsic River and the Maine Central and Canadian Pacific rail lines, eliminating two railroad crossings.

C.H. & GEORGE H. CROSS CO. DELIVERY TRUCKS, late 1930s. The Cross Co. bakery business produced many varieties of bread and cakes which were delivered to stores throughout the area, but their widely-known specialty, as the sign indicates, was the delicious large round crackers known far and wide as St. Johnsbury Crackers. These were perfect for crackers and milk, and enjoyed an excellent mail-order demand.

PERLEY RUSSELL'S ICE WAGONS, 1905. The demand for ice in St. Johnsbury, before the advent of the electric refrigerator, amounted to some 10 tons a day in warm weather, and selling it became a thriving business. Perley Russell bought this going concern, located at the foot of Hastings Hill, from Mark Hovey in 1903.

THE A.H. MCLEOD MILLING CO., *c.* 1920. In 1871 Angus McLeod acquired this mill, located on the site of Jonathan Arnold's first mill in St. Johnsbury, and McLeod constantly enlarged and improved it. It was purchased and further improved in 1910 by Jonas and Alfred Brooks, and became Caledonia Mills, Inc., in the 1920s. The next owner was the Ralston Purina Company, which operated at that location until wartime shortages of construction materials eased enough to permit the construction of a new mill.

THE RALSTON PURINA COMPANY MILL, 1948. Ralston Purina's fine new building provided facilities for the manufacture of Purina Chows for all of New England. People watched with interest the construction of the elevator on concrete pillars 16 feet deep, and were particularly entertained when the construction workers put a lighted Christmas tree atop the 150-foot-high structure, making it the highest Christmas tree in Vermont!

TURNER CENTER CREAMERY, 1920s. This creamery building, one of the finest in the area, was built in 1919 by the Plymouth Creamery and sold in 1926 to Turner Center Systems of Maine. In 1929 H.P. Hood & Sons acquired it, and over the next twenty years they enlarged the facilities and put in fine equipment, in order to produce their entire ice cream supply for northern New England, which was delivered from here by a large fleet of trucks.

BARROWS CHAIR FACTORY, 1930s. Built by Manton-Gaulin Co. for manufacturing dairy equipment in 1926, this building was acquired in 1936 by Fred W. Barrows, who started a furniture manufacturing business which continued on into the 1950s under various owners. In 1959, in a sharp change, it became St. Johnsbury's first discount department store—Ames, which brought a new concept in shopping.

THE CARY MAPLE SUGAR CO. AND MAPLE GROVE CANDIES, 1930. George Cary, whose dealings in maple sugar gave St. Johnsbury its claim to being the Maple Sugar Center of the world, built his four-story factory in 1920. Nine years later, after he and Earl Franklin had purchased the Maple Grove Candies manufacturing business, the big brick Maple Grove factory was built in the same area on the east side of town.

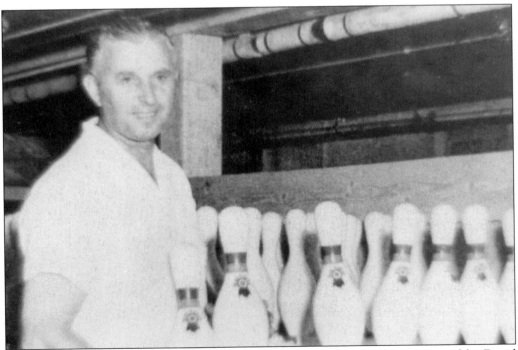

THE TEMPERED MAPLE CORP., 1950s. The Tempered Maple Corp., operated by David Finklestein, moved to St. Johnsbury in 1936 and became the largest manufacturer of bowling pins in the world. It operated here until 1958 under the management of Philip Iverson (shown here), and turned many, many of our maple trees into bowling pins, to satisfy the great interest in bowling at that time.

ST. JOHNSBURY GLOVERS, 1950s. This firm, which manufactured very fine quality ladies' gloves, started operations here in 1943, and built their factory on lower Railroad Street in 1949. By 1952, their "Crescendoe" gloves were featured on the cover of *Life* magazine, and operations were in high gear. This photograph shows the workers very briefly on strike, as part of the ILGU. The two interesting houses in the background are no longer in the area.

THE NEWEY BROS. FACTORY ON WARREN'S FLAT, 1960. The purpose of this small manufacturing building, constructed in 1959 just east of town, remained a mystery until it actually opened in mid-April. The tenants were a Canadian firm called Newey Bros., who manufactured small sewing items like hooks and eyes, zippers, and needles. It never became a large employer, but it did remain in business, under its British-born managers, for quite a number of years. Many children found the British accents of the managers and their families quite enjoyable.

C.H. GOSS CO. EMPLOYEES MAKING SANDPAPER TIRES, 1940s. In the 1940s, the C.H. Goss Co. started the production of winter tires made on retreads with the addition of a surface containing sand. These were most effective for winter driving in this part of the country, as well as being quite inexpensive, and they sold very well.

A TRUCKLOAD OF TIRES FROM TEXAS FOR THE C.H. GOSS CO., October 1958. The C.H. Goss Co.'s sandpaper tires became so popular that they could not get a sufficient supply of old tires to retread, and they had to buy a large truckload of these from Texas which, of course, has large amounts of everything.

Two
Fairbanks' Cultural Contributions

ST. JOHNSBURY ACADEMY, 1880s. St. Johnsbury Academy, founded in 1842 by Erastus, Thaddeus, and Joseph Fairbanks, became the special interest of Thaddeus, who contributed the two fine brick buildings known as North Hall (1873) and South Hall (1872), which served as the school for more than fifty years.

THE ATHENAEUM UNDER CONSTRUCTION, early 1869. The Main Street-Eastern Avenue corner is shown here cleared of buildings, in preparation for the construction of the large brick block that went up on that site. The Athenaeum, in progress since 1868, looks quite well finished, but the detailed interior work and the acquisition of its fine books postponed the official opening until November 1871, when Horace Fairbanks donated it to the people of St. Johnsbury as a free public library.

THE NEW ATHENAEUM WITH MR. THAYER ON ITS STEPS, 1872. Every detail of trim on the mansard tower and the balconies shows up well on the newly-completed Athenaeum. The gentleman in the tall silk hat is the Reverend W.W. Thayer, who married the widow of Joseph Fairbanks and became the first librarian at the Athenaeum.

24

THE INTERIOR OF THE ART GALLERY, 1930s. Soon after the Athenaeum was completed, work commenced on an addition at the rear designed to showcase the huge Albert Bierstadt painting *Domes of the Yosemite*, which Horace Fairbanks had been able to acquire with the help of John Davis Hatch, the architect of the Athenaeum. Mr. Fairbanks devoted much time and attention to collecting paintings for this fine collection, which emphasizes the Hudson River School of painters.

TOUCHING UP THE DOMES, May 1957. During Albert Bierstadt's lifetime, he made almost-yearly trips to St. Johnsbury to visit his fine masterpiece, but after his death the Athenaeum had to arrange for occasional "first aid" for the great painting. This was a 1957 touch-up.

THE MUSEUM UNDER CONSTRUCTION, 1891. The Fairbanks Museum of Natural Science, a munificent gift from Franklin Fairbanks to the people of St. Johnsbury, had its cornerstone laid in July 1890. It was about a year later, on June 17, 1891, that the last stone was hoisted to the top of the tower. The dedication ceremonies, upon completion of the interior, were held on December 15, 1891. It was a very snowy evening, but St. Johnsbury people, who had been eagerly awaiting a look at this wonderful gift, turned out in large numbers to enjoy its wonders.

THE COMPLETED FAIRBANKS MUSEUM, 1900. It became apparent within a short time after the opening of the Museum that more space was needed to display the tremendous collections which Franklin Fairbanks had acquired. In 1894 an extension of the south side of the building was made, bringing the Museum to its present impressive appearance.

THE LIVE MUSEUM WITH SCHOOLCHILDREN, May 1960. Fred Mold was almost as much interested in animals as he was in children, and one of his particular interests was acquiring live animals who could be taken care of on the Museum grounds by his junior curators, who learned many lessons about responsibility as well as biology.

FRED MOLD AND GROUNDHOG, c. 1955. In 1948 the Fairbanks Museum acquired the most important addition ever made to its collections—a man named Fred Mold, who came to St. Johnsbury to take over the directorship. Fred dedicated himself completely to bringing the Museum back to life and using and improving its facilities for the benefit of the young people of the area. This is Fred with his groundhog at the weather station on February 2, Groundhog Day.

OPEN HOUSE AT THE MUSEUM, January 1960. As the Museum came to life under Fred Mold's leadership, people came in increasing numbers to view the changes and improvements being made in their Museum. The annual open house gave the townspeople an opportunity to see how the place was changing and broadening its appeal.

THE YMCA BUILDING, 1900. The Young Men's Christian Association had been active in St. Johnsbury for many years, without a home of its own, when Reverend Henry Fairbanks, son of Thaddeus, decided to build a fine structure for the group on upper Eastern Avenue. This was finished in 1885, and was another of Lambert Packard's architectural achievements.

THE NORTH HALL FIRE, March 6, 1956. On Town Meeting Day in 1956, North Hall of St. Johnsbury Academy suffered a devastating fire. However, the efforts of the students—who made innumerable trips up and down the three flights of stairs—saved a large part of the books and equipment, and work got underway promptly on Ranger Hall, a fine replacement.

ST. JOHNSBURY ACADEMY, 1960. From left to right, Ranger Hall, Colby Hall, and Fuller Hall made up the impressive, up-to-date St. Johnsbury Academy of 1960.

Three
Celebrations, Sports, and Pastimes

JUMBO PETS ON PARADE, 1885. St. Johnsbury people had the opportunity to see many circuses through the years. Many were at the Fairground, located a mile south of the main business district, but the parades on Main Street were always a major attraction. P.T. Barnum's famous Jumbo appeared here on August 12, 1882, and took his third American bath in the Passumpsic River, below the Fairground.

CAPTAIN ED GRISWOLD'S BALLOON *AEOLUS* AT THE CALEDONIA COUNTY FAIR, 1894. Captain Griswold, a well-known St. Johnsbury resident, took a hot air balloon ride in 1891, and decided he wanted a balloon of his own. This was finally completed in 1894, and on September 12 of that year he made an ascension at the Caledonia County Fairground, staying aloft for 75 minutes and landing in Bethlehem, NH, some 25 miles away.

HORSE RACING AT THE FAIR, 1895. Harness racing has always been one of the big attractions of the Caledonia County Fair. Huge cavalcades of oxen, horses, sheep, and calves were held, as well as fine displays of flowers, vegetables, fruits, and handwork in Floral Hall.

THE CALEDONIA COUNTY FAIR, 1895. A county fair was held each year on the Caledonia County Fairgrounds, which were acquired in 1859. Originally the fairs were held in October, but eventually the dates were moved back into somewhat warmer weather. However, attendance declined in the late 1920s, and in 1930 the Fairground property was sold to St. Johnsbury Academy for an athletic field.

A PARADE AT THE MAIN STREET CORNER, 1896. This appears to be mainly a parade of decorated bicycles, especially those of young people. Bicycles were all the rage for many seasons in the late 1800s, and one reads of races to nearby towns, with new records being set each year. There was even a bicycle path project which made some progress one year. History does repeat itself!

MUSIC HALL, LATER THE COLONIAL THEATRE, 1900. The old North Church, moved to the corner of Church and Main Streets, was given by Horace and Franklin Fairbanks to the YMCA to be used for their lecture and concert programs. The public, in 1884, subscribed $14,000 to convert it to a fine hall, which was used for many years. First called Music Hall, it later became the Colonial Theatre, and burned in 1924.

THE RIVERSIDE CANOE CLUB, 1910. The Canoe Club was organized in 1908 and became a very popular spot where canoes could be rented for the 5-mile round trip to St. Johnsbury Center. A tragic drowning accident in 1912 took three young lives and dampened the canoeing spirit, but the club continued to operate until the 1927 flood washed it away.

THE OLD PINE TENNIS CLUBHOUSE, 1910. Old Pine was a popular spot for golf and tennis from the early 1900s until the 1950s, boasting the best clay tennis courts in Vermont. Its fine view, overlooking the town, made it a popular gathering spot for young and old.

PRESIDENT TAFT SPEAKING AT THE ATHENAEUM, October 10, 1912. President Wm. H. Taft, running for re-election in 1912, came to St. Johnsbury in an auto cavalcade for lunch at Underclyffe mansion and a parade through the decorated town. He spoke to a very large crowd from a platform at the Athenaeum. The car in the foreground belonged to Elmore T. Ide.

CAMELS PARADING BY THE MUSEUM, 1912. One of St. Johnsbury's many circus shows brought these camels parading by the Fairbanks Museum, along with a group of elephants who were carrying advertisements for a boys' clothing sale at Moore & Johnson's store.

THE AMERICAN LEGION AUXILIARY DRUM CORPS, 1930s. The local American Legion post, named for W.R. Knapp, St. Johnsbury's first casualty of World War I, was formed in 1920. The men had a drum corps of sorts in the late 1920s, but gave up on it, and a few years later their wives, the Auxiliary, took over and made fine appearances in many parades.

THE ST. JOHNSBURY COUNTRY CLUB, 1926. Local golf enthusiasts, led by Dr. Frank Farmer, took advantage of an opportunity in 1923 to purchase the Maplewood Stock Farm, just north of St. Johnsbury Center, and create a fine 9-hole golf course. The farmhouse was remodeled into an attractive, up-to-date clubhouse in 1926.

FAIRBANKS CENTENNIAL HEADQUARTERS AT THE ARMORY, 1930. In 1930 the 100th anniversary of Thaddeus Fairbanks' invention of the platform scale, which started the E. & T. Fairbanks Co. on the road to fame and riches, was celebrated on the July Fourth weekend. A huge parade, and a pageant with appropriate scenes showing the growth of the firm into a world-wide operation, made the weekend a memorable one. The National Guard Armory on Main Street served as the center of operations.

THE DEDICATION OF THE ARNOLD MARKER, July 4, 1930. A suitably-inscribed marker indicating the site of the original home of the man who founded St. Johnsbury—Jonathan Arnold—was dedicated by two Arnold descendants, Claude Arnold and Lyndon Arnold. The location is Arnold Park, at the head of Main Street.

THE STAR AND PALACE THEATRES, 1936. Lower Eastern Avenue was the location of these two movie theatres, where many townspeople found their best relaxation. Both theatres were built in late 1926 and were well-patronized. The Palace had a fine organ to add class to its programs, and a vaudeville show every week. The Star had fewer amenities, but had a balcony, a favorite with teenagers. Going to the movies, during the Depression and war years, was a fine way to pick up one's spirits and forget problems for a time.

SWIMMING POOL FUN, 1945. With our nearest lake some 10 miles away, St. Johnsbury people, young and old, had long wished for a place to cool off on a hot day. In 1943 that wish was fulfilled with a fine swimming pool, built and still maintained under the aegis of our local Kiwanis Club.

KIDS IN THE ARNOLD PARK FOUNTAIN, 1947. On a hot day, this was a simple way to cool off for the little kids who were too young to go to the big swimming pool. Mothers found it a blessing.

THE KING REID CARNIVAL BEING SET UP, 1947. There was always excitement when the carnival came to town, and the King Reid show was a Vermont one that people were glad to support. The kids were delighted to watch it being set up, down on Gilman Field.

THE KING REID CARNIVAL, 1947. Always there was the question: what rides were going to be running—swings, airplanes, the ferris wheel? And of course there were always games of chance, where you might win a doll, a teddy bear, etc. You might—or might not.

A RAILROAD STREET BAND CONCERT, 1949. St. Johnsbury's town band, the third oldest in the entire USA, provided the townspeople with fine concerts on summer Sunday nights. The concerts alternated between Main Street and Railroad Street. This was a favorite place for young and old alike. After all, who knew whom you might see and maybe get to walk home with?

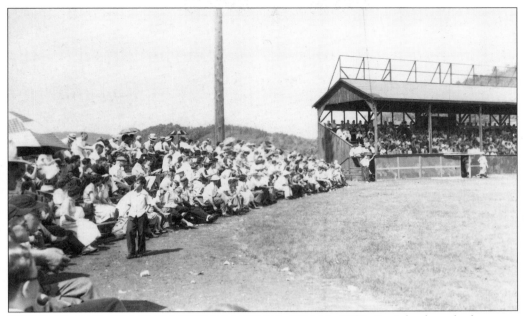

OPENING DAY FOR THE TOWN BASEBALL TEAM, 1950. St. Johnsbury had a town baseball team for many years. Although it was an expensive proposition, local businessmen were generous with their support and our St. Johnsbury Senators (later the Tri-County Yankees) found many fans. They played at Hazen Field.

OPENING DAY FOR LITTLE LEAGUE BASEBALL, May 1952. Little League baseball, sponsored by the Rotary Club, got off to a great start. This has added much to the spring and summer months for over forty years, both for kids and their parents.

THE KING BROS. CIRCUS PARADE, July 18, 1951. The parade moves along Railroad Street in front of familiar storefronts, with the usual crowd of onlookers to enjoy the elephants—not really a novelty anymore, but always an attraction.

A CIRCUS TENT ON GILMAN FIELD, July 18, 1951. This is probably the last circus tent on Gilman Field. Soon thereafter, the field was graded to be used for Little League baseball, sponsored by the Rotary Club, spearheaded by Dr. Bill Robinson, whose concern for youth was a great benefit to our local youngsters.

A SOAPBOX DERBY ON WESTERN AVENUE, July 11, 1951. This exciting event, sponsored by the Rotary Club, brought out some fine race cars, whose drivers maneuvered their gravity-propelled vehicles down the steep pitch skillfully. Notice the beautiful elm trees.

ANOTHER VIEW OF THE SOAPBOX DERBY ON WESTERN AVENUE, July 11, 1951. As these contestants await their turn, one can admire the fine houses in the background, which were later removed to make room for the Streeter Hall building.

FRESH AIR KIDS ARRIVE, 1952. This program for disadvantaged kids from New York City brought dozens of youngsters here to spend two weeks in an atmosphere where they could enjoy green fields, farm animals, and fresh air. This particular year they came by train.

FRESH AIR KIDS DEPART, 1952. The final goodbyes at the station were always a little sad, after making new friends, but many children came back another year or even for Christmas.

ROTARY YOUTH BASKETBALL,
December 1952. The basketball program for
grades six through eight was sponsored by the
Rotary Club, with the uniforms and
equipment financed by local businesses. This
proved to be a healthy and enjoyable way to
occupy winter months.

ROTARY BASKETBALL, 1952. The coaches for the Rotary teams not only developed a fine
relationship with their players, but greatly improved the quality of the talent going up into St.
Johnsbury Academy.

FOUNTAIN GIRLS AT THE PARKER DRUG STORE, 1947. One of the pleasures looked forward to each day by the downtown workers was getting a lemon or cherry coke at Parker's on the way home. These were the smiling faces of good friends.

BUYING AN EASTER BONNET, 1956. At the time, an Easter bonnet was a pleasant necessity for girls and ladies, and this wall of hats in Hovey's Shops provided ample choice. How quickly the millinery business faded, when the rule requiring heads to be covered in church was removed! The glove market, closely related, also suffered.

Four

For Freedom
and Country

TROOPS HEADING OFF FOR THE KOREAN CONFLICT, August 4, 1951. These soldiers were photographed in the doors of a train as it passed through St. Johnsbury.

THE CIVIL WAR: THE 3RD VERMONT REGIMENT ON MAIN STREET. This group of Vermont men, trained at our local Camp Baxter, left for the war on July 24, 1861, on a train of twenty-two cars. They comprised 888 men from various parts of Vermont, who had received basic training at a hastily-constructed facility at the local Caledonia County Fairground.

THE 3RD REGIMENT BAND, July 24, 1861. This twenty-four-man regimental band went off to war with their regiment. These men provided music for morale, but also had duties as stretcher bearers, in times of conflict. In August 1862 bands were dismissed from the army, and they returned to St. Johnsbury.

WILLIE JOHNSTON, A MEDAL OF HONOR WINNER, 1862. St. Johnsbury took great pride in this thirteen-year-old drummer boy who went to war with his father, William Johnston, a member of the 3rd Vermont Regiment. In the Peninsula Campaign, when soldiers were retreating in great disarray, Willie brought his drum off with him, the only drummer to do so. For this, he received the Congressional Medal of Honor in September 1862.

THE SOLDIERS' MONUMENT IN COURTHOUSE SQUARE, 1868. This fine monument, dedicated in St. Johnsbury on August 20, 1868, bears the names of all the St. Johnsbury men who died in the Civil War. The white marble statue, called *America,* was sculpted in Italy by Larkin Mead, a Vermont sculptor. Gilmore's Band provided music for the dedication.

THE SEND-OFF OF COMPANY D TO THE SPANISH-AMERICAN WAR, May 6, 1898. A huge crowd saw Company D of the Vermont National Guard off to the Spanish-American War. The large parade featured bands, local lodges, and organizations, and at the railroad yard speeches were given from a platform. The men were sent on their way with cheers and torpedoes.

COMPANY D AT THE NEW ARMORY, 1916. The new National Guard Armory was completed on Main Street in 1916. These members of Company D, posed on the steps, were to take part in World War I, and were part of the one hundred members of the Guard who left on April 6 for Fort Ethan Allen. On July 25 they officially became part of the U.S. Army.

THE "WAKE UP, AMERICA" PARADE, April 1917. Shortly after the United States declared war on Germany, the largest parade ever seen in St. Johnsbury took place, with over three thousand people marching, to show their support for the war. Signs were carried, urging people to raise food and support the President.

THE "WAKE UP, AMERICA" PARADE, April 1917. This section of the parade, led by Spirit of '76 characters, made a fine impression. Most of Main Street was jammed with spectators.

THE "WAKE UP, AMERICA" PARADE, April 1917. This section of the parade featured six local doctors, followed by the entire Brightlook Hospital nursing staff. Perhaps it should be explained that the partly-visible "Hookers for Humanity" sign refers to a local machine shop called Hooker's.

THE "WAKE UP, AMERICA" PARADE, April 1917. The business section of Main Street, by the St. Johnsbury House, was a sea of people and interesting automobiles when this photograph was taken. Enthusiasm was really whipped up by this gigantic parade.

THE CROWD TO GREET RETURNING SOLDIERS, 1919. Hundreds of people on the sloping banks of Railroad Street Park await the arrival of soldiers. Familiar signs on the businesses in the background include Tinker's Quick Lunch, long a landmark, and A.E. Counsell Co., which dealt in Harley-Davidson motorcycles.

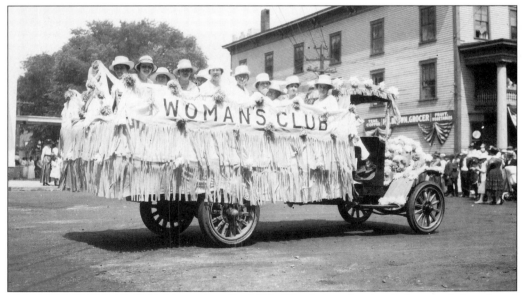

THE VICTORY PARADE, November 11, 1918. Word that the Armistice was being signed precipitated a grand parade which included decorated floats. This one was adorned with several members of the Woman's Club, a fine group responsible for the beautification of parks, the municipal forest, drinking fountains, watering troughs, and many other projects.

COMPANY D ON THE ARMORY STEPS, 1941. Company D of the Vermont National Guard was mustered into federal service on March 12, 1941, and left for Camp Blanding, Florida. They had been "living" at the Armory since February, and it was actually a relief to be on their way at last. Their top officers were already away for special training. You may recognize Bill Cutting and Floyd Heath, in the center row, along with many other friends.

COMPANY M OF THE VERMONT NATIONAL GUARD, OFF TO CAMP PICKETT (KOREAN CONFLICT), September 11, 1950. Company M is shown here marching to the railroad station to entrain.

FAMILIES AT THE RAILROAD STATION. These families await the departure of the train with Company M members on board. One little child is being held up for a last hug and kiss from his father.

A FINAL GOODBYE. A father, mother, and little girl were photographed while saying their final farewells near an express cart at the station.

A TROOP TRAIN HEADING FOR DANVILLE, June 26, 1956. This was the longest train ever to operate on the St. J. & L.C. Railroad, with a total of twenty-four cars and six locomotives. It had nineteen Pullman cars, two baggage cars, two milk cars, and one coach, weighing a grand total of 2,030 tons.

Five
Trains, Trucks, and Automobiles

A COLLISION AT THE RAILROAD STATION, April 1960. This car took on a little more than it could handle when it ran away and collided with a train at the railroad station. The freight car was the clear winner.

AN EARLY ST. JOHNSBURY & LAKE CHAMPLAIN LOCOMOTIVE, 1880s. The Maquam, built in 1872 in Taunton, MA, became part of the St. J. & L.C. Railroad in 1890, when that line was created to take over the Vermont division of the Portland & Ogdensburg Railroad.

A ST. JOHNSBURY & LAKE CHAMPLAIN LOCOMOTIVE, early 1900s. Boston & Maine No. 32 was built in Schenectady, NY, in 1898. This Class C-16A was leased to the St. J. & L.C Railroad.

THE ST. JOHNSBURY ROUNDHOUSE AND TURNTABLE, 1890s. This structure was built in 1888, after a fire destroyed the previous one. It held fifteen locomotives.

REBUILDING THE MAINE CENTRAL RAILROAD BRIDGE NEAR PORTLAND STREET, 1905. This covered bridge over the Passumpsic River replaced the original 1871 structure. It was solidly built and served until the flood of November 1927, when it had to be burned in order to eliminate the chance of its being swept against the highway bridge next to it and wiping that out.

LOCOMOTIVES IN THE ST. JOHNSBURY RAILROAD YARD, late 1940s. At left is a Maine Central engine; at right, a St. J. & L.C. switching engine.

A DERAILMENT IN THE RAILROAD YARD, April 1952. Several box cars in the St. Johnsbury yard, near the Ide Co., were knocked off the track during this accident.

A CLOSER VIEW OF THE DERAILMENT SCENE, April 1952. This closer view, showing interested spectators, allowed us to identify brakeman Maurice Drown (squatting at left).

A STUDY IN CONTRASTS, 1950s. Faithful old No. 27, the St. J. & L.C. Railroad's last steam engine, stands beside one of the newer diesel engines—No. 49—which replaced her.

CANADIAN PACIFIC'S DAYTIME PASSENGER TRAIN, 1940s. The Alouette, which made the run from Montreal to Boston, was an express put into service in 1926 to meet the competition from automobiles. It is shown here speeding toward Boston, south of St. Johnsbury by the gas plant. There was also a night express, called The Red Wing.

CANADIAN PACIFIC'S DAYTIME PASSENGER TRAIN, 1950s. The Alouette acquired a
fine new diesel engine to up-date and improve its service, in a rather hopeless effort to make the
railroad competitive with the automobile.

A ST. JOHNSBURY TRUCKING COMPANY TRUCK, 1929. At this point, much of the company business was moving household goods, in this type of van.

THE ZABARSKY BROTHERS, mid-1950s. Shown here are, from left to right: Maurice (the executive vice-president), Milton (the secretary-treasurer), and Harry (the president). They built their corporation to its peak, spreading the name of St. Johnsbury over the entire eastern U.S. It was always a thrill to meet one of their trucks when one was far from home.

1920 *Safety First Pays — Drive Carefully* **1937**

ST. JOHNSBURY TRUCKING CO.
BONDED F REIGHT FURNITURE FORWARDERS

PORTLAND OFFICE AND TERMINAL	**MAIN OFFICE**	BOSTON OFFICE AND TERMINAL
73 MAIN ST. SO. PORTLAND TEL. 2-0722	**and WAREHOUSE**	46 CARLETON ST. CAMBRIDGE, MASS.
		TEL. TROWBRIDGE 6050
BARRE OFFICE AND TERMINAL.	76 Portland St. St. Johnsbury, Vt.	
SMITH ST. TEL. 884-W	TEL. 602	WELLS RIVER TERMINAL
BURLINGTON TERMINAL TEL. 153	NEWPORT TERMINAL PHONE 370	MAIN ST. TEL. 143

MODERN, SAFE AND FAST REFRIGERATED FREIGHT SERVICE

One Of The Several Most Modern Type Trailers Used By The St. Johnsbury Trucking To Transport Perishables Rapidly And Safely Over Long Distances.

One Of The 10 Wheel Refrigerator Trucks Used By The St. Johnsbury Trucking Company To Carry Perishable Merchandise Quickly And Safely To Its Destination.

Long Distance Moving Specialists
Using Modern Padded Vans

**S
H
I
P

B
Y

T
R
U
C
K**

FIRST
FROM STANDPOINT OF
EQUIPMENT IN
NEW ENGLAND

SECOND LARGEST
NUMBER OF TRUCKS IN
VERMONT
40 TRUCKING
UNITS

REGISTERED
UNDER THE
INTERSTATE
COMMERCE
COMMISSION

COMPLETE
WAREHOUSE AND
DISTRIBUTION
SERVICE

ALL GOODS
INSURED
IN TRANSIT

No Need To Worry About Your Furniture When It Is Packed In One Of The St. Johnsbury Trucking Company's Roomy Vans By Their Expert Packers And Movers. They Move You Quickly, Safely And Economically. Expert Packing Service If Desired.

DAILY SERVICE
TO AND FROM
BOSTON
AND
NEW ENGLAND
POINTS

REGULAR SERVICE
TO SPRINGFIELD
CONNECTICUT CITIES
AND NEW YORK
ALSO
PORTLAND
AND ALL PARTS OF MAINE

LOCAL SERVICE
TO BARRE
BURLINGTON
NEWPORT, WHITE RIVER
AND ALL
VERMONT POINTS

DOOR TO DOOR
SERVICE

Heavy Hauling and Construction Service

Tractors, Trailers and Trucks Of All Description Enable The St. Johnsbury Trucking Co. To Handle The Heaviest Hauling, Construction Work Etc. With The Same Ease and Efficiency That Its Fine Equipment Gives In Other Branches Of The Trucking Business.

A ST. JOHNSBURY TRUCKING COMPANY ADVERTISING SHEET, 1937. The company had grown considerably by this time, from its beginnings in 1921, when Harry and Mickey Zabarsky had one old truck that they used between St. Johnsbury and Boston whenever they could find a customer for their services.

A ST. JOHNSBURY TRUCKING COMPANY TRUCK, 1950. The new 1950 mode of transportation is parked in front of the Portland Street terminal in St. Johnsbury.

A ST. JOHNSBURY TRUCKING COMPANY TRUCK IN AN UNDESIRABLE POSITION, December 27, 1950. An interested audience views a mishap near the railroad station. Fortunately, the smoke is from a locomotive.

THE FAIRBANKS BLOCK ON MAIN STREET, 1954. This historic building in a fine location was purchased in February 1954, and renovated to become the St. Johnsbury Trucking Company headquarters.

A NEW 1958 ST. JOHNSBURY TRUCKING COMPANY VAN, 1959. This impressive vehicle at the St. Johnsbury terminal has been identified as part of the United Van Line moving fleet.

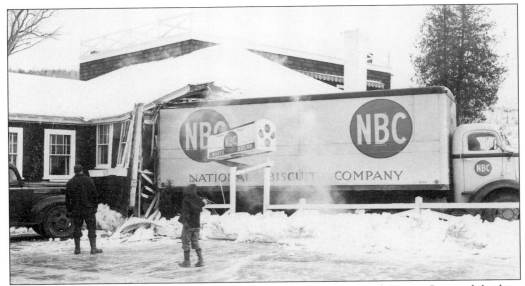

A DIFFERENT KIND OF DELIVERY, February 1951. This National Biscuit Co. truck broke a shifting lever on the hill beyond Aime's, and ended up 7 feet inside Aime's Restaurant, just east of St. Johnsbury.

TWO GENTLEMEN OUT FOR A SPIN, *c.* 1900. This elegant automobile, displaying features like rear fenders, a chain-drive mechanism, a steering tiller, fine headlights, and a front trunk for storage, was obviously the "last word" at that point.

GOING TO THE FAIR, 1901. Here we have the old and the new, entering the Caledonia County Fairgrounds. The two buggies were still the usual way to travel. The new-fangled automobile attracted a good deal of attention, because it was a real novelty.

A NEW 1903 STANLEY STEAMER, 1903. Charlie Simanton, the local dealer for the Stanley Steamer, posed with his wife and sons in this family model, which had a passenger seat in front.

THE C.H. GOSS CO. GARAGE ON CENTRAL STREET, 1910. C.H. Goss was one of the first Packard dealers in the country. His interest in automobiles was originally sparked by Buffalo Bill Cody's use of one in the parade preceding Cody's Wild West Show here in July 1896.

THE 1911 ST. JOHNSBURY AUTOMOBILE SHOW, May 10, 11, and 12, 1911. This show, which took place at the Goss Co. garage, is said to have been the first in a long succession of annual auto shows here. These were held at the Armory in later years.

THE WARREN MOTORS DEALERSHIP ON PORTLAND STREET, 1947. This new building, located at the corner of Concord Avenue, was put up in 1946 and early 1947 by members of three generations of the Warren family: James, Harold, and Richard. The Warrens also acquired the Studebaker dealership at that point.

THE NORTHERN CADILLAC CO.'S NEW SALES AND SERVICE BUILDING, 1957. This new and modern structure on U.S. Route 5, north of town, was completed and opened in June 1957. Their clever sign features "The Long and Short of It"—a fine new Cadillac luxury town car, and a very small Renault.

ADAMS B. SCOTT, A LONG-TIME TAXI MAN, August 9, 1948. Adams B. Scott is shown here standing by his taxi, in front of his home on Portland Street. He had served St. Johnsbury people for many years, meeting all of the day and night passenger trains, but by this time his wife was doing most of the driving.

Six

Serving the
Traveling Public

THE ST. JOHNSBURY RAILROAD STATION, 1908. Built in 1883, this elegant station served Canadian Pacific, Maine Central, and St. J. & L.C. Railroad traffic. This familiar view shows what most passengers first saw as they came into St. Johnsbury. For many years, passengers using the east-west lines had to cross the main line tracks, which were nearer the station.

THE ST. JOHNSBURY HOUSE, *c.* 1910. The St. Johnsbury House, our best-known Main Street hostelry, was built in 1850, and had a gable roof similar to other buildings in that area.

THE ST. JOHNSBURY HOUSE, 1920s. The old hotel was taken over by a group of St. Johnsbury businessmen in 1914. A complete renovation created a four-story, flat-roofed building with a columned front porch, modern accommodations, and a fine dining room in the large ell that was added. This familiar building served the public for over fifty years after this photograph was taken.

THE ST. JOHNSBURY HOUSE LOBBY, early 1900s. This lobby is quite typical for a hotel which catered largely to the traveling salesmen of the time. One sees advertising calendars, what appear to be train schedules for the railroads which served the town, and also a public telephone.

THE OLD AVENUE HOUSE, early 1890s. This hotel, which dominated the Railroad Street business area, started life as the Passumpsic House in 1850, when the first railroad passenger trains came into St. Johnsbury on the Connecticut & Passumpsic Rivers Railroad. In 1868 it was greatly enlarged to the size shown here and renamed the Avenue House. The neighboring Howe Opera House was built in 1891.

AFTER THE AVENUE HOUSE FIRE, January 1896. A disastrous fire completely destroyed the hotel, with the loss of one life. Several of the downtown businessmen invested in rebuilding, and we acquired the distinctive towered New Avenue House, the centerpiece of the Railroad Street business area from then on.

THE NEW AVENUE HOUSE, *c.* 1915. Originally there was a cigar store in the corner room, and a fine cigar store Indian stood on the steps. However, in 1916 the hotel office was moved into the circular room and a very attractive balcony was built out over the sidewalk, sheltering many people from sudden showers.

LETTERING IN THE RAILROAD STREET PARK, 1900. The white stone lettering on the slope facing the railroad station was put there in the 1890s by the Woman's Club, and met with much favorable comment from visitors arriving by train. The area where the horse and buggys stand was put to that use for many years, even after automobiles dominated parking.

THE DEPOT RESTAURANT, early 1900s. For a great many years this location was a familiar and handy place for railroad passengers to eat. This particular restaurant, called the People's Restaurant, was operated by Allison & Davies. Oysters, a very popular dish here, got special mention, and the ICE CREAM TODAY sign seems to indicate it was not always available.

THE ST. JOHNSBURY STEAM LAUNDRY ON RAILROAD STREET, *c.* 1910. During the time of stiff collars for gentlemen, laundry care was really required. Apparently business was good enough to require the fancy delivery wagon parked in front.

AN INTERIOR VIEW OF THE ST. JOHNSBURY STEAM LAUNDRY, *c.* 1910. The number of shirts being laundered, starched, and ironed is quite clear. Today's well-dressed males can be grateful that this fashion has departed from the scene.

THE MAPLE GROVE INN, 1920s. "Pinehurst," the beautiful mansion built by Horace Fairbanks in 1852, was purchased in 1920 for use by Maple Grove Candies. At first they used part of the building for making the popular maple candy products. After a factory was built in 1929 in another part of town to take care of the candy production, the mansion became a fine inn and tea room.

THE STAFF AT MAPLE GROVE, 1920s. A group of Maple Grove workers surround Katherine Ide Gray, head of the Maple Grove Candies operation. They produced delicious confections which found a ready market around St. Johnsbury, in their New York City tea room, and literally world-wide, in a mail-order business.

THE SOUTH END SERVICE STATION, 1931. A typical Gulf service station, built according to Gulf's standard plans, opened in 1931 on South Railroad Street (U.S. Route 5). Proprietor Arthur Schoppe and his son Maurice dispensed gasoline and oil, sold Century tires, and repaired and sold Grunow radios and refrigerators. In 1931, making a living was not easy.

Seven

Our Taxes at Work

THE ST. JOHNSBURY TOWN FARM, early 1900s. St. Johnsbury first set up a town farm, for the care of paupers, in 1837. A much better house was built in 1854, along with a number of barns and sheds, so the place could be a self-sufficient farm. Many residents were elderly or disabled. Young people, fatherless or orphaned, were apprenticed out to local farmers who, in exchange for their services until the age of twenty-one, provided food, lodging, clothing, a good elementary school education, and training in operating a farm. Girls were taught to be farmers' wives. This system worked very well, both for the farmers and the children.

AN OLD ROAD SCRAPER, 1890s. In the late 1800s, the job of keeping gravel roads in smooth condition was done by this type of road scraper, pulled by four horses—a four horsepower piece of equipment, you might say. St. Johnsbury had a goodly amount of road mileage to maintain; the official figure in 1893 was 95 miles, which meant a lot of scraping.

A SNOW ROLLER, 1890s. In 1888 Beauman Butler built the first snow roller in the area, for a neighboring town; St. Johnsbury acquired one for use on the main roads, and one for use on the streets. In 1904 it was reported that St. Johnsbury had seven heavy snow rollers in the town barn, along with seven iron-gray horses to pull them.

A SNOW LOADER BY THE NEW AVENUE HOUSE, 1946. In 1928 St. Johnsbury finally decided roads had to be plowed, but this left huge piles of snow by the streets. People thoroughly approved of the purchase of a Barber-Greene snow loader in 1946, and promptly named her "Barbara Greene." She attracted many onlookers, as in this December 1946 scene.

A SNOW LOADER ON SUMMER STREET, 1956. As the years passed, improvements were made in snow-loading machines. This blower-type snow loader is shown here cleaning up Summer Street.

THE NEW STREET SWEEPER, 1949. Streets needed care in the summer, also, and in 1949 St. Johnsbury acquired a fine new street sweeper to clean up the dust and trash. Municipal Manager Sumner displays it here proudly. Store owners were asked to sweep after work so the night rounds of the sweeper could pick up the dirt.

THE NEW GARBAGE TRUCK, 1949. Another very helpful municipal service was the collection of garbage. This is the new garbage truck, delivered in March 1949, and again we have Manager Sumner alongside the driver, as they pose with what came to be called "The Salad Bowl."

PART OF THE VILLAGE FIRE DEPARTMENT, early 1900s. Before St. Johnsbury had a central fire station, each area had its own volunteer firefighters. Hose Company No. 6 was located on Concord Avenue near Portland Street. When they were called out, Myron Simpson's big horse was hitched up for duty. This was a real improvement over earlier days, when the men had to pull these big wagons to the fire themselves.

THE FIRST FIRE TRUCK, AT THE EASTERN AVENUE STATION, 1915. The town bought this American LaFrance fire truck in May 1912, and installed it in an Eastern Avenue structure built for that purpose. With 70 horsepower, it was guaranteed to climb any hill in town at 48 mph. This was the first fire station with quarters for firemen, and it served as the fire station until the new municipal building was completed in May 1923 on Main Street. The driver is Henry Juneau.

THE NEW FIRE TRUCK, 1949. In July 1949 the town acquired a new Pirsch-Ford fire truck. It was a 500-gallon-a-minute pumper with chemical fog apparatus, reportedly one of the first in the country to have this equipment. Familiar faces include Hubert Simons (behind the wheel), Howard Penniman and Claude Arnold (near the truck), and "Lady," the fire dog who understood both English and German.

UNLOADING THE NEW FIRE TRUCK, July 1949. The fine new truck came in by rail, and was unloaded near True Temper Corporation's place of business, off Portland Street.

LONGTIME FIREFIGHTER HUBERT SIMONS, 1950s. Hubert Simons, who was first the assistant fire chief and then fire chief, is shown here hard at work on an aerial ladder.

FIREMEN REPAIRING TOYS IN THE FIRE STATION, 1950s. One of the fine contributions of our fire department is the work done in repairing donated toys, which are then distributed to underprivileged children of the area. This particular year had a bumper crop of sleds, wagons, and bicycles for the firemen to work on. Identified are Bernard Perkins and John Willey (in front), and Ernest Leclerc and Hubert Simons (at rear).

THE POLICE DEPARTMENT, 1920s. This brings nostalgic thoughts of a time when a three-man police department took good care of St. Johnsbury. Hopefully, people will remember Tom Wallace, John Finley, and George Short, who worked twelve-hour shifts, seven days a week—one man in the station and the other two on the street.

THE POLICE DEPARTMENT, 1950s. Here we have Chief Bill Burgess and his eight-man force. From left to right are: Floyd Easter, George Wilkins, Poly Faucher, Ben Shafer, Chief Burgess, Ray Kittredge, Bert Boutain, Jim Piper, and Gerry Coburn. They worked a sixty-hour week, with a day off, and the department acquired a cruiser and radio communication. People had changed.

A GRADUATION AT THE SUMMER STREET SCHOOL, 1898. Schools were very much a part of our tax picture, from the earliest days. The people who graduated from ninth grade at the Summer Street School in 1898 had an informal photograph taken, bicycles and all, near the front of the North Building. Some of them have been identified: Mabel Woodside, Mabel Spencer, Emma Swanson, Raymond Pearl, Charles Flint, and William Bemis.

SUMMERVILLE SCHOOL, 1900. Summerville School, now called the Portland Street School, was designed by local architect Lambert Packard and opened in April 1900. In this photograph, three teachers can be seen in their ground-sweeping skirts, model attire for the times.

THE NEW TRADE SCHOOL, 1942. The St. Johnsbury Trade School, the first four-year trade school in Vermont, opened in 1942 and earned a fine reputation. Large numbers of its graduates found good jobs in defense industries, especially in Connecticut.

THE JUNIOR HIGH ADDITION, 1953. With the local elementary schools bursting at the seams, an addition to the St. Johnsbury Trade School was completed in 1953. The addition provided classrooms for all seventh and eighth graders in town, as well as a fine new gymnasium. The gymnasium was dedicated with a concert by the U.S. Marine Band, which was enjoyed by a capacity crowd.

93

THE NEW SCHOOL BUS, 1958. St. Johnsbury acquired its first school bus in October 1958— a Ford, which gave good service for many years. This has since been joined by many more of the familiar yellow vehicles which transport elementary students to the in-town schools.

A NINETY-NINE-YEAR-OLD VOTER, November 1960. People in Vermont take their voting privilege seriously. This is ninety-nine-year-old Amy Jones, using her absentee ballot, which has been delivered by Justices of the Peace Hugh Impey (Democrat) and Leonard Goss (Republican).

THE VERMONT BOOKWAGON IN FRONT OF THE ATHENAEUM, 1959. Turning to state, rather than local taxes, one fine benefit for the smaller schools in the area, which do not have large libraries, is the Vermont Bookwagon, a traveling library which is eagerly welcomed by rural school students.

THE NEW POST OFFICE BUILDING, 1924. In 1924, Uncle Sam provided St. Johnsbury with its first U.S. Post Office building, a real step up from the rented quarters which had been used for so many years, and outgrown. This fine brick building on Eastern Avenue, just above the Masonic Temple, served us well for forty-one years.

THE HIGHWAY POST OFFICE, 1958. One more federal innovation was this Highway Post Office, seen here parked on Eastern Avenue across from the Ellis Paint & Wallpaper Store. It was equipped to pick up mail all along the main routes, and sort it en route, as railway post office cars had done for many years. It went into service in September 1958. Postmaster Frank Barney is the gentleman in the light suit.

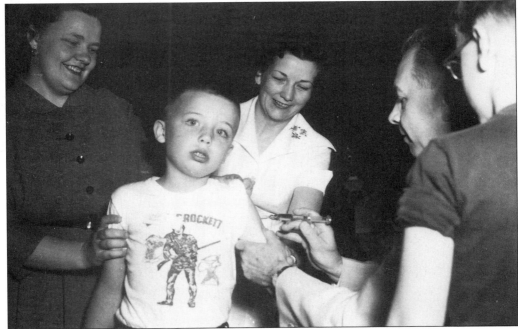

THE FIRST POLIO VACCINE SHOTS, 1955. The Salk vaccine was an answer to the prayers of parents who had lived with fear of a polio epidemic during August and September of every year. The first shipment arrived here in May 1955, and our schoolchildren were promptly vaccinated. Dr. Howard Farmer is shown here giving the shot to a little boy, who is trying to keep a stiff upper lip.

Eight

Weather: Its Pleasures and Problems

KIDS PLAYING IN SNOW AT VETERANS ROW, 1947. Snow provides a lot of fun for youngsters, and one place which had a lot of youngsters was the Veterans' Row government housing project, put up on Elliott Street in 1946, when there was a desperate shortage of housing for the young families of returning war veterans.

A BOYS' ASSOCIATION SLEIGHRIDE, 1876. A group of forty boys, from ten to fifteen years old, was formed in 1876 by Colonel E.P. Farr, who met with the boys on a weekly basis to try to improve their lives. This outing was a trip by sleigh to East St. Johnsbury, where the boys met in the church with local people, sang songs, were spoken to by the Honorable Calvin Morrill, and generally had a fine time.

THE OLD CLINTON AVENUE TOBOGGAN CHUTE, 1887. St. Johnsbury joined the tobogganing fad in 1887, forming a club and raising money to have this large structure built from Clinton Avenue to the Summer Street Common. Crowds of people, young and old, used it. Being on private property, it had to be dismantled in the summer, and when it was put up again the next winter, there was not enough interest to maintain it. It was a short-lived fad.

THE OLD PINE TOBOGGAN CHUTE, 1920s. By the early 1920s there was an active winter sports club in town, led by Dr. Dale Atwood. Membership buttons admitted one to the skating rink and the ski trails and toboggan chute at the Old Pine Sports Club. This chute lasted for several years.

A SNOW SCENE ON CHURCH STREET, early 1900s. Local professional photographer Katherine Bingham loved winter scenes, and a big snowfall always had her out taking pictures. This particular view was taken at the end of a driveway on Church Street, with snow piled up nearly to the height of the ladies who are out looking over the landscape.

A SNOW SCULPTURE AT ST. JOHNSBURY ACADEMY, 1951. The Winter Carnival at the Academy has always been a February highlight, and through the years there have been many fine sculptures for people to enjoy. This 1951 example shows the amount of effort which went into creating these for the inter-class competition.

A ST. JOHNSBURY ACADEMY SNOW SCULPTURE, 1951. Sometimes more efficiency can be achieved with something other than shovel and muscle; it is always handy if some parent has machinery which can be borrowed.

THE LINCOLN STREET SKI TOW, January 1960. Beginning in 1957, on the property bought as a site for the Lincoln Street School, there was an area on which a good rope ski tow could be set up. This gave the young people of town a chance to learn to ski, without the expense of traveling to a resort.

FLOODING THE RINK AT GILMAN FIELD, 1948. In the winter of 1948, the town's severe water shortage made it impossible to spare enough water to flood the usual three neighborhood skating rinks. A practical solution was found: use a hose to take water from the Passumpsic River to flood Gilman Field, and let everyone skate there. This required much time and effort, but was accomplished by Chet Buck, the longtime Portland Street rink caretaker, who is shown here with Municipal Manager Sumner.

KIDS AT THE PORTLAND STREET SKATING RINK, January 1951. These young people are having a fine time skating at the Portland Street rink. The buildings in the background, some no longer there, include Harry Dolgin's big store block, which housed the First National Store.

A SNOW BLOWER ON UPPER MAIN STREET, 1950s. This snow blower is clearing the street in front of some fine Main Street homes: the Flint house (1870) is at the left; the 1820 Paddock mansion is in the center; and the 1874 Henry Clay Ide house is at the right.

THE ST. JOHNSBURY CENTER ICE JAM, 1915. An incredibly destructive ice jam occurred in St. Johnsbury Center on February 25, 1915. Chunks of ice piled up in the streets made travel impossible for several days, wiping out the Bacon bridge and leaving huge towers of ice by the side of the road. The gentleman in the buggy is in a position to show how high one of the towers was.

THE ST. JOHNSBURY CENTER ICE JAM, 1915. This little girl is standing in front of the familiar two-story yellow home in the center of the village, which belonged to the Chaffee family for many years. It is the most impressive of a long row of 1850s houses in the Center village.

THE FLOOD OF 1927, NEAR ARNOLD'S FALLS, November 4, 1927. At the peak of the 1927 flood, torrents of water poured over the Passumpsic River dam near the Arlington bridge. All of the factory buildings shown have since been destroyed by fire, but two of them have been replaced, and they look much the same. The small building in the foreground has survived, although it is empty at present.

ST. JOHNSBURY CENTER, November 5, 1927. The main street (U.S. Route 5) in St. Johnsbury Center was badly washed out by the flood and many house foundations were ruined, but even the most badly-damaged home, referred to as the Tipsy House for obvious reasons, has been back in use ever since.

BRIDGELESS ST. JOHNSBURY CENTER, November 5, 1927. One of the Center's important landmarks is missing in this photograph, taken on the day after the great flood. Fortunately it ran aground a short distance down the river, and was replaced within a month, for many more years of use.

THE HURRICANE OF 1938, September 21, 1938. September 1938 brought to this part of New England the only honest-to-goodness hurricane ever. A violent storm hit the southern coast in Rhode Island and continued northward, roaring through the Connecticut River valley in its full fury. St. Johnsbury village lost seventy-five trees. This one found a dormitory to lean against, on St. Johnsbury Academy property.

THE 1948 WINDSTORM. On June 24, 1948, a powerful storm hit. For a short time it rivaled a hurricane: we had hail and a cloudburst of rain, along with tremendous winds which downed ten large trees, knocked out six hundred telephones, and left a real mess at Cross and Pearl Streets, where seven trees crashed down and crushed Howard Suitor's car quite flat.

Nine

The Changing Face of St. Johnsbury

RAILROAD STREET, early 1870s. These two large brick blocks at the south end of the business district, on the east side of Railroad Street, are the Ward Block (on the right, where the Citizens Bank is now) and the Flanders Block (purchased in the 1880s by Merchants Bank and later rebuilt by that bank). Note the steps up to the "street-level" stores, and the steps down to the "basement-level" stores.

A VIEW OF THE MUSEUM SITE FROM THE COURTHOUSE ROOF, 1870s. This view is looking toward the Prospect Street area, where the Fairbanks Museum would be built some twenty years later. The church steeple is the old North Church, from which the South Church was copied. The gabled block at the left appears to be the Brown Block, before it became flat-roofed following an 1893 fire. In the foreground is Eastern Avenue, and the big white tenement building just over the chimney is the Armington Block, later torn down to clear the site for the Museum.

UPPER EASTERN AVENUE, 1870s. In the center is the new Athenaeum. Two buildings on the upper portion occupy the site where the YMCA Block would be built. The block at the right edge is the Fletcher hardware store, which was later moved up Prospect Avenue when the Pythian Block was built at that corner in 1893. The left-hand side of the street, now occupied by Palmer Bros., is very empty.

AN EARLY VIEW OF THE EAST SIDE OF MAIN STREET, 1880s. This is mainly familiar territory: the big brick block, built in 1869, still looks the same, and the Brown Block (at left) is still in place. The smaller block has been removed and replaced. Note the plank sidewalk to help pedestrians cross the dirt street, and the wagon parked right across it.

A VIEW ACROSS EASTERN AVENUE TO NOTRE DAME CHURCH, 1890. Notre Dame Church (at left) was built in 1888, and in 1893 the large house seen near Notre Dame was purchased by the Roman Catholic Diocese, to be used for the care of the poor and sick. It was shortly replaced by St. Johnsbury Hospital, which opened in 1895. On Eastern Avenue in the foreground is the square Wakefield Block, then five small buildings and the large Gauthier Block, now Town House Apartments, flanked by the Universalist church building, which is no longer in existence.

THE PYTHIAN BLOCK AND AREA, 1890s. The Pythian Block, the finest Pythian lodge building in the state at that point, was built in 1893, but burned the next year. It was rebuilt in 1896, and has since changed little, except that the tower has been removed. At the right, across Prospect Avenue, is what began in 1891 as the Presbyterian church. It eventually became a commercial block: at the time of this photograph, it was the Central Quick Lunch, but later it became a fine furniture store, then a printing establishment, and is now Aja's Pizzeria.

A CONVERSATION ON MAIN STREET, 1890s. This situation, with two elderly gentlemen, well-dressed and obviously men of character, differing strongly in their opinions, must have been repeated many times on Main Street.

ORVILLE LAWRENCE BY STEELE'S STORE, 1890s. Orville was a "town character" who had made a fortune on Wall Street in the late 1860s as the partner of Russell Sage, but lost it all in the Panic of 1873. He came back to Waterford to farm. Orville was quick-witted and outspoken, and many entertaining stories have been told about him.

THE SOUTH CHURCH, IN A VIEW TO THE NORTH, 1870s. This typical white New England church is flanked by the Academy's North Hall (to the right) and an Academy boarding house (to the left). The brick sidewalk and the fine fence, typical of the time, add much to the appeal of the scene.

ST. ANDREW'S EPISCOPAL CHURCH. Erected in 1878, St. Andrew's was one of the churches built on Main Street in the 1870s. Having been started in November, the construction crew was very fortunate to have good weather all the way through January, with men working in their shirtsleeves. It is a stick-style building, and was designed by W.P. Wentworth of Boston.

M. E. Church, St. Johnsbury, Vt.

THE SECOND METHODIST CHURCH, 1890s. The original Methodist church, built in 1856, was the first non-Congregational church on the Plain. In 1883 the Methodists needed a larger church and built this structure with the tall steeple.

THE FIRE AT THE METHODIST CHURCH, 1915. In January 1915 a devastating fire, undetected for quite a while because of the slate shingles on the steeple, destroyed the church. This picture was taken before the steeple fell.

THE NORTH CONGREGATIONAL CHURCH, 1881. This impressive gray stone church was built on Main Street, largely through the generosity of Horace and Franklin Fairbanks, who covered all costs involved over and above the $37,000 which the parishioners had been able to raise. Obviously the beautiful Isle LaMotte limestone building cost a great deal more than that amount.

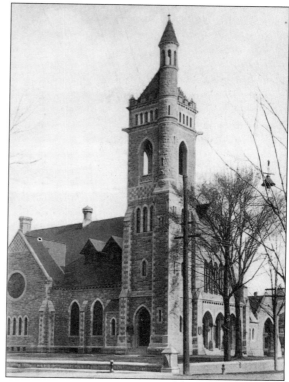

"DR. BOB'S" HOUSE, c. 1890s. Located on the corner of Summer and Central Streets, this building is the birthplace and boyhood home of "Dr. Bob," co-founder of Alcoholics Anonymous, who graduated from St. Johnsbury Academy in 1898. In recent years the home was purchased by present-day members of the organization. It has been nicely renovated, and is currently used by A.A.

THE GREAT RAILROAD STREET FIRE, 1892. On Sunday afternoon, October 27, 1892, a terrible fire erupted in the Caldbeck Block, which wiped out everything on the east side of Railroad Street as far north as the Johnson Block, as well as the Griswold & Pearl grain store by the railroad station. To orient yourself: the fence at the lower right encloses Railroad Street Park, and lower Eastern Avenue runs across the lower part of the scene.

THE STATUE OF "HOPE," 1893. M.J. Caldbeck, who owned the Caldbeck Block, promptly rebuilt after the fire, as did the other block owners. Mr. Caldbeck installed this fine statue of "Hope" over the entrance to his building, in memory of an employee who died in the fire. The statue was made by Carrick Brothers, a local granite firm which did fine statuary work sold in many parts of the country.

THE WILLOUGHBY DINER, 1937. The Willoughby Diner, built on Eastern Avenue just north of the two theatres, became a favorite rendezvous of workers in the business district, as well as theatre-goers who desired a good piece of pie and a cup of coffee after the show. Lloyd McKee, the genial owner, believed in good food and good service, and when good help was unavailable, he sold the place. Later owners had less success than Mac.

MOVING THE WILLOUGHBY DINER, June 1959. In 1959 the good old Willoughby started on a journey to a different part of town. Moved in two sections by the St. Johnsbury Trucking Co., it ended up on Portland Street, where it has since remained, first having served food, and recently having sold books—food for the mind, as it were.

117

THE GRAND OPENING OF THE NEW FIRST NATIONAL STORE, September 1955. The fine Fairbanks Dry Goods Store, built in 1890, has had many owners through the years. It became Brooks-Tyler's in 1897, then Berry-Ball Dry Goods, Cooney Furniture, and Curran Furniture, before being leased by the First National Store in 1955. In September 1955, First National had a grand opening. This was their finest store north of Laconia, NH, and they offered great bargains. Look at the price of ice cream!

MAIN STREET BY THE EASTERN AVENUE CORNER, *c.* 1930. The new traffic light at the top of Eastern Avenue and the big old elm tree on the lawn of the Municipal Building are noticeable features which help to date this very familiar scene.

C.H. STEVENS' HOUSE ON MAIN STREET. Built in 1890, this beautiful Queen Anne-style home, designed by Lambert Packard for C.H. Stevens, a lumber baron, continues to attract visitors who admire fine architecture.

THE NORTH END OF MAIN STREET, 1950. The beautiful vista created by the lovely old elm trees which almost met over the north end of Main Street was one of the finest in Vermont. Unfortunately, we lost the elms to disease, but the homes are still a treasure to appreciate.

Ten
Our Extended Communities

MAIN STREET, EAST ST. JOHNSBURY, 1926. This car is coming down the hill into the village, on the old gravel road. The road has been much improved, but the three houses on the left and two on the right are quite recognizable, and look much the same today as they do here.

THE OLD TANNERY AND BRIDGE, 1907. The old covered bridge across the Moose River, in the center of East St. Johnsbury, was a constantly-used part of the village for many years. In 1926 it caught fire and was destroyed, being replaced shortly thereafter by the present concrete structure. The tannery, which had been there since the 1820s, is long gone.

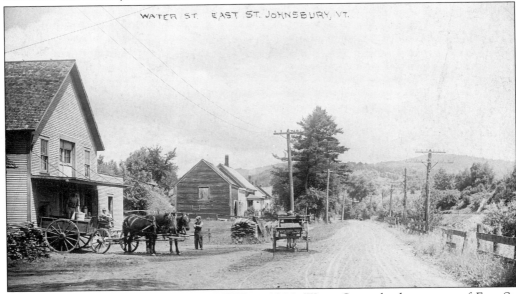

AN EARLY VIEW OF WATER STREET, c. 1914. Water Street leads east out of East St. Johnsbury village. The message on the back of this postcard tells us that the youngster sitting on the beam is young Hugh Ramage.

WATER STREET, 1920s. The general store is on the in-town part of Water Street in East St. Johnsbury. Your magnifying glass will reveal that this large building is the U.S. Post Office, has a pay station for the Passumpsic Telephone Co., and sells Daniel Webster Flour.

THE EAST ST. JOHNSBURY SCHOOL, 1930s. In December 1926, the East St. Johnsbury School became the first rural school in Vermont to get a Superior School designation, for meeting the standards set by the Vermont Board of Education. It still stands, as a part of Peter and Polly Park, in the village.

HALLOWE'EN IN EAST ST. JOHNSBURY, 1950. Hallowe'en trick-or-treating on October 31, 1950, brought out these kids, dressed in their best costumes and masks. Perhaps they will recognize themselves.

THE OLD ST. JOHNSBURY CENTER MEETINGHOUSE, early 1900s. This building was built in 1804 on a hill west of the Center village, as St. Johnsbury's first meetinghouse. In 1845, due to a shift in population, it was taken apart and reconstructed at this location as the First Congregational Church, which is still an active organization.

A ST. JOHNSBURY CENTER RIVERSIDE VIEW, mid-1920s. The placid Passumpsic River, flowing past the St. Johnsbury Electric Co.'s fine building and dam, gives us a pleasant contrast to the more familiar view of devastation created by the 1927 flood at this spot.

ST. JOHNSBURY CENTER, 1930. The bandstand and general store are decorated for a 1930 celebration. The John A. Chalmers IGA store is dispensing Esso gasoline. Notice the ingenious arrangement, with extensions of the gasoline hoses to the street edge, so cars would not have to go on the sidewalk.

THE ST. JOHNSBURY BAND, NEAR THE CENTER BANDSTAND, 1930s. St. Johnsbury's fine town band is lined up prior to giving a concert in St. Johnsbury Center. It appears that the bandstand has been moved back from the roadside location where it was earlier shown.

THE CENTERVALE STATION AND BRIDGE, 1920s. People in St. Johnsbury Center crossed the iron bridge to reach the railroad station. Note that the railroad's name for the village was Centervale. The other sign is for the Western Union telegraph service. This bridge was washed downriver in the 1927 flood but later retrieved.

THE GREEN MT. GRANGE IN ST. JOHNSBURY CENTER, 1926. The Green Mt. Grange No. 1 building is decorated for a 1926 celebration. This was, as it says, the first Grange in New England, chartered on July 4, 1872. By 1926 the Grange had been able to purchase and remodel this building for its purposes.

MAIN STREET (U.S. ROUTE 5), 1920s. The St. Johnsbury Center village has changed little over the years. At this point, Elmore H. Chase's general store is also the post office, and has a pay station telephone. The Center Garage across the way sells Socony gasoline and motor oil, and the pump farther down the street belongs to Texaco. One of the noticeable features shown is a very large elm tree. Some years later, this fell across the road and created a major traffic jam on Route 5.